Contents

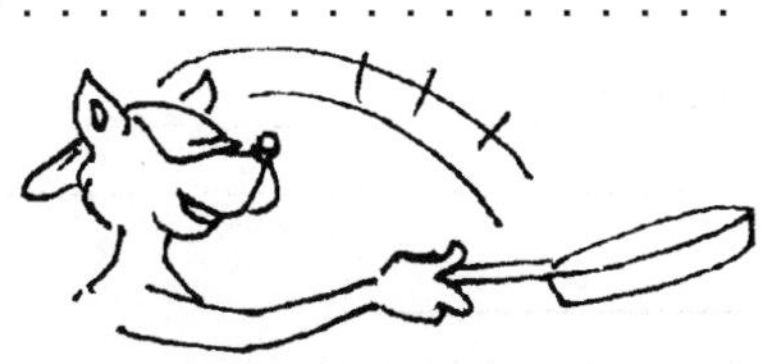

Sally's birthday

PIN THE TAIL ON THE DONKEY

Hello, Sally.
Great!
Let's play a party game.
Terrific!
Happy birthday to you. Happy birthday to you.
How old are you today?
Let's sing a birthday song for Sally.
I'm eleven.
Hello, Mrs Smith. It's my birthday today.
Oh yes!
We can play "Pin the tail on the donkey."

Now you can sing this birthday song with your classmates!

Match the verses to the pictures and colour the pictures.

Happy birthday to you!

Happy birthday to you,
Happy birthday to you,
Happy birthday, **dear Sally,**
Happy birthday to you!

1. Lots of presents for you,
   Lots of presents for you,
   Because it's your birthday,
   Lots of presents for you!

2. Here's a nice card for you,
   Here's a nice card for you,
   Because it's your birthday,
   Here's a nice card for you!

3. There is ice-cream and jelly,
   There is ice-cream and jelly,
   Because it's your birthday,
   There is ice-cream and jelly!

4. There are lots of balloons,
   There are lots of balloons,
   Because it's your birthday,
   There are lots of balloons!

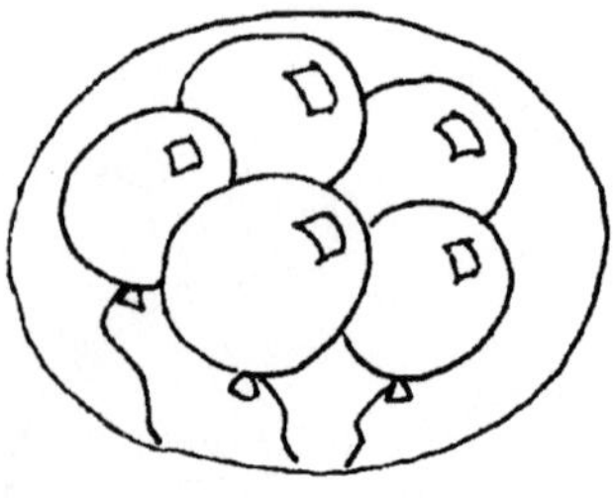

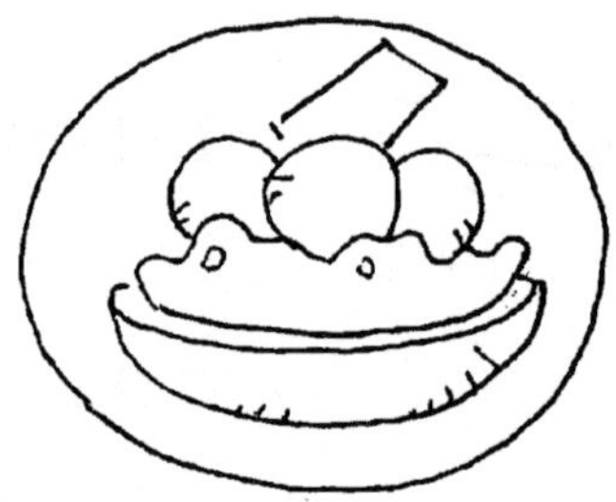

5. Let's play lots of games,
   Let's play lots of games,
   Because it's your birthday,
   Let's play lots of games.

It's Sally's birthday party today.
Look at the picture of her living-room.
Now read the text and finish the picture.

Sally's birthday party

birthday cake

candles

plate

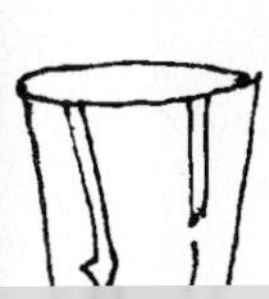

It's four o'clock. Sally's birthday cake is on the table. There are eleven yellow candles on the cake. There are four plates, four glasses and two bottles of lemonade on the table, too.
Sally's cat Minny is on a chair. There are three balloons under the table. Two big red balloons and one little green balloon. Sally and her three friends are in the garden. Sally's dog Spot is in the garden, too. He has got a black and white football.

balloons

football

Pin the tail on the donkey - an English party game

Look! This is a picture of a big donkey.

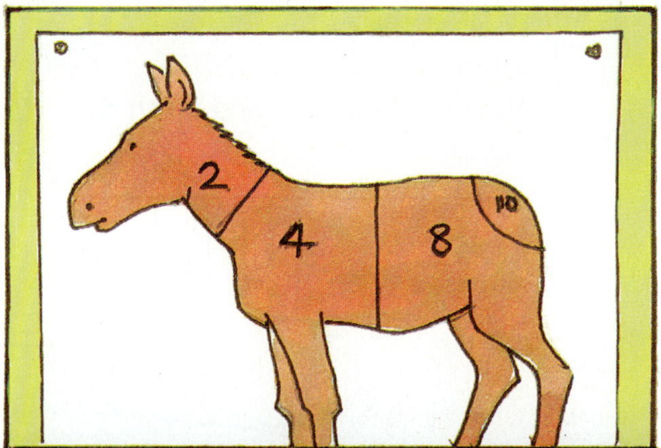

There are numbers on the donkey.

The donkey hasn't got a tail.

Here it is! Sally has got the donkey's tail. She has got a drawing-pin too.

Here's a blindfold for Sally.
Now she can't see the donkey.

Turn Sally....
one-two-three.

Come on Sally! Pin the tail on the donkey!
Sally must pin the tail on the donkey.
??
The tail is on the donkey. It's on the donkey's head.
POINTS
SALLY 2
TIM
JOHN
JANE
ROBERT
That's two points for you Sally.
Sally has got two points. Now it's Tim's turn.
Thanks.
Here you are, Tim.
Here you are, Tim. Here's the tail with the drawing-pin and blindfold.
Ten points. Super!
Two points. Bad luck!
How many points have you got?
I've got four points.
It's my turn!
Twenty points. Tim is the winner!
Turn Tim...one-two-three!
Pin the tail on the donkey!

Now play the game with your classmates!

HALLOWEEN
31ST OCTOBER

Here is a song about Halloween.
Find the words for the pictures in the song. Write the words under the pictures.

k. ______________

a. ______________

1. Witch and princess, ghost and monster,
   Walking down the street.
   Walking down the street.
   Children knocking at the door
   Shouting 'Trick or treat!'
   Children knocking at the door
   Shouting 'Trick or treat!'

j. ______________

b. ______________

2. Look what I've got in my bag,
   Apples, chocolate, sweets! *(2 times)*
   Let us go from house to house
   Shouting 'Trick or treat!' *(2 times)*

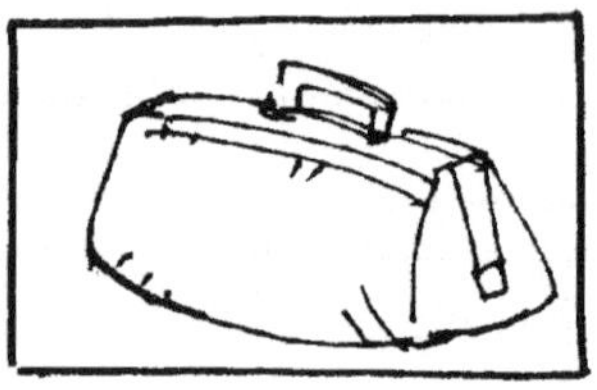

i. ______________

c. ______________

3. Now let's have a spooky party
   With games and things to eat. *(2 times)*
   Pumpkin faces, bats and broomsticks -
   Tonight is 'Trick or treat!' *(2 times)*

(Tune: "Fuchs du hast die Gans gestohlen")

h. ______________

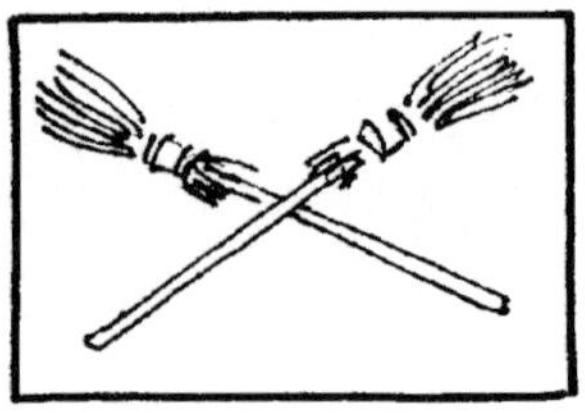

d. ______________

e. ______________

f. ______________

g. ______________

Make a vampire bat

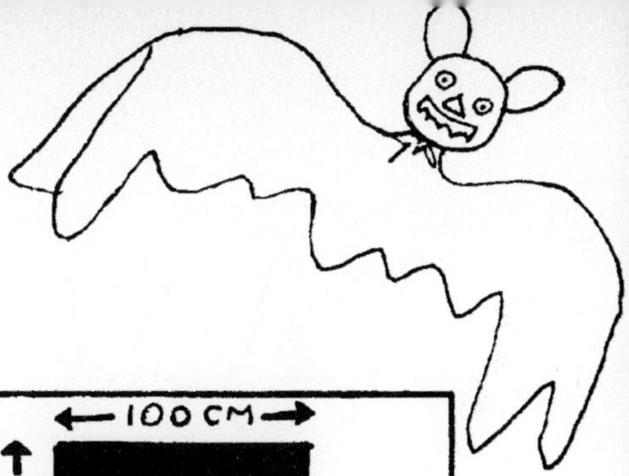

You need:

- some scissors 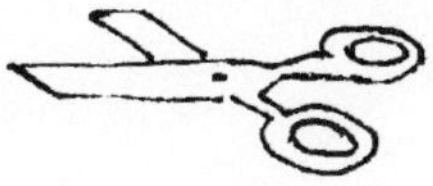
- some glue 
- a wire clothes hanger 
- an old tennis ball 
- some soft, black material 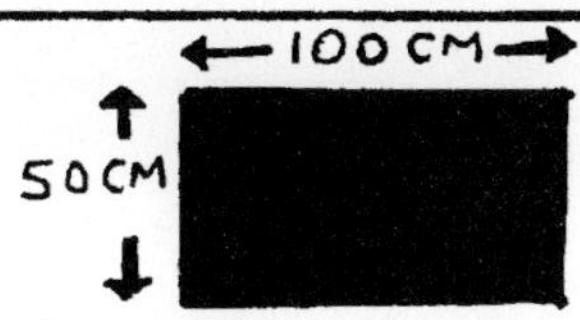

- some black thread 
- a sharp knitting needle 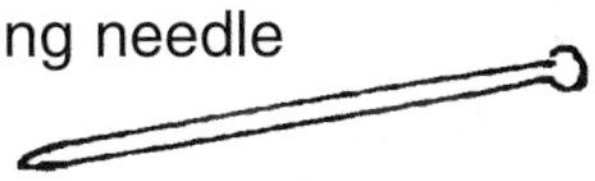
- 2 eyes, a nose and vampire teeth (white paper)

Bend the wire clothes hanger - like this:

These are the bat's wings!

Make a hole through the tennis ball. Then push the ball into the hanger.

This is the bat's head!

Now fold the black material in half, then in half again. Cut a *very small* piece from the folded corner.

Push the top of the wire hanger through this hole.

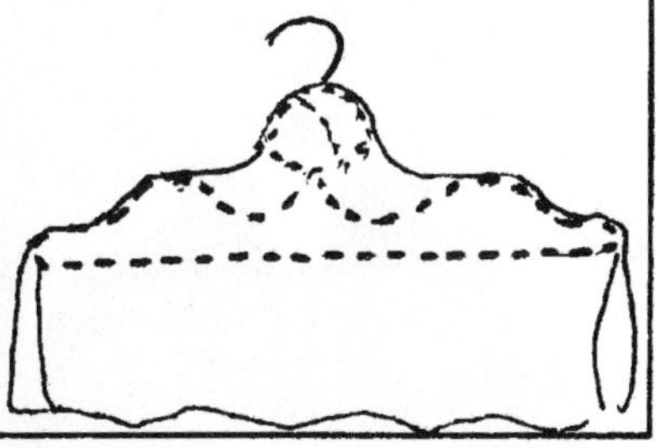

Now form two big ears on the head. Tie them with black thread.

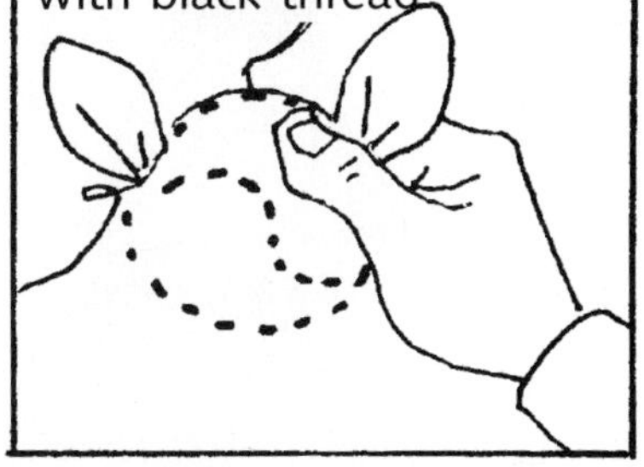

Next form the head - like this.

Cut the material to form bat wings.

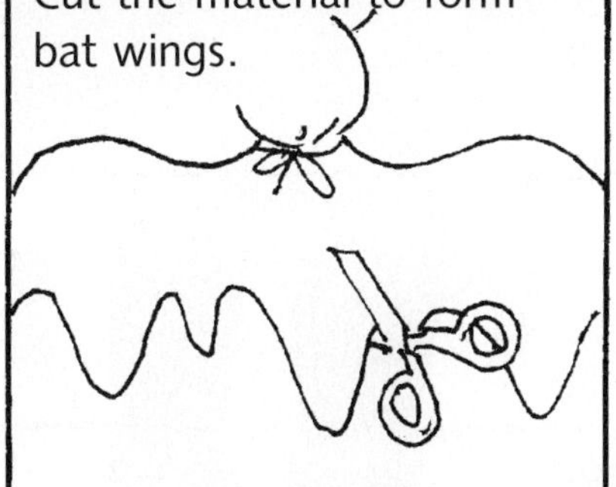

Last of all give the bat two eyes, a nose and vampire teeth.

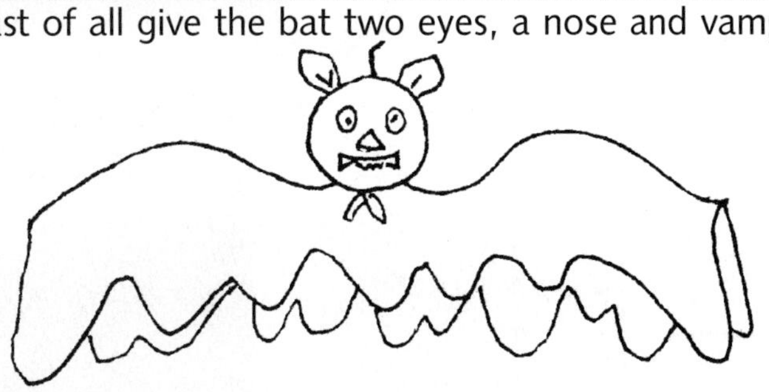

Now your vampire bat is finished!

The boys and girls in Sally's class are having a Halloween party at school. Look at their Halloween costumes and then read the notes on the pinboard. Who is what?
Can you complete the sentences on page 11?
OUR COSTUMES FOR HALLOWEEN
I've got ... - a golden crown - a pink dress - golden shoes What am I? Sally
I've got ... - big black eyes - a big mouth - a white sheet What am I? Danny
I've got ... - a tall black hat - a long nose - a long black dress - a broomstick What am I? Jenny

1. Susan is a ____________________.
2. Tim is a ____________________.
3. Sally ____________________.
4. Danny ____________________.
5. Jenny ____________________.
6. Henry ____________________.

monster
witch
vampire
cat
ghost
princess

TRICK OR TREAT? A HALLOWEEN STORY

First look at the pictures.
Then look at the pumpkins at the bottom of each page.
Now write the story about Sally and Tim under the pictures.

1.

2.

3.

4.

TRICK OR TREAT?
5.
OOOHH!! WHOOOH! THIS IS FOR YOU!!
Help! A ghost!
6.
What is in the bag, Tim?
Yuck! It's a trick. It's slime!
7.
Ha! Ha! Ha! Ha!
Look at the ghost! It's Danny!
8.

Tim is looking in the bag. There's some cold, green slime in the bag.
Tim can see the ghost at the window. The ghost is Danny!

Let's play a trick on Danny the ghost!
4
9.
4
TRICK OR TREAT?
10.
OOOHH! WHOOOOO!!! WHO'S THERE??
11.
Here you are Danny. Here's a nice trick for you!
OH NO! SLIME!! YUCK!!
12.

Now the green slime is on Danny's head.
Sally and Tim are at the door of house number four again.
Danny the ghost is opening the door.
Sally has a good idea.

It's Christmas time!

You can colour this picture.

Father Christmas is wearing a red coat  and a red hat. 

His face  is pink and his beard  is white.

He has got green gloves  and his sack  is brown.

It's night time and the stars  are yellow.

A song about Father Christmas

(Tune: Bruder Jakob)

Father Christmas, Father Christmas;
He got stuck, he got stuck
Coming down the chimney,
Coming down the chimney,
What bad luck!
What bad luck!

It's Christmas Eve. Sally, Ben and Mark are upstairs in bed. They are sleeping. Their Christmas stockings are hanging by their beds. Little Mark is dreaming. Father Christmas is coming down the chimney with a big sack of Christmas presents.

Mum, Dad and Spot are downstairs in the living-room. The living-room is very pretty. There are lots of Christmas cards on the wall. There are coloured paper-chains hanging from the ceiling.

Mum and Dad are listening to Christmas carols. Dad is singing, too! Spot is sitting under the Christmas tree. He is barking at the coloured fairy lights. They are going on - off - on and off.

C____t____ _a_

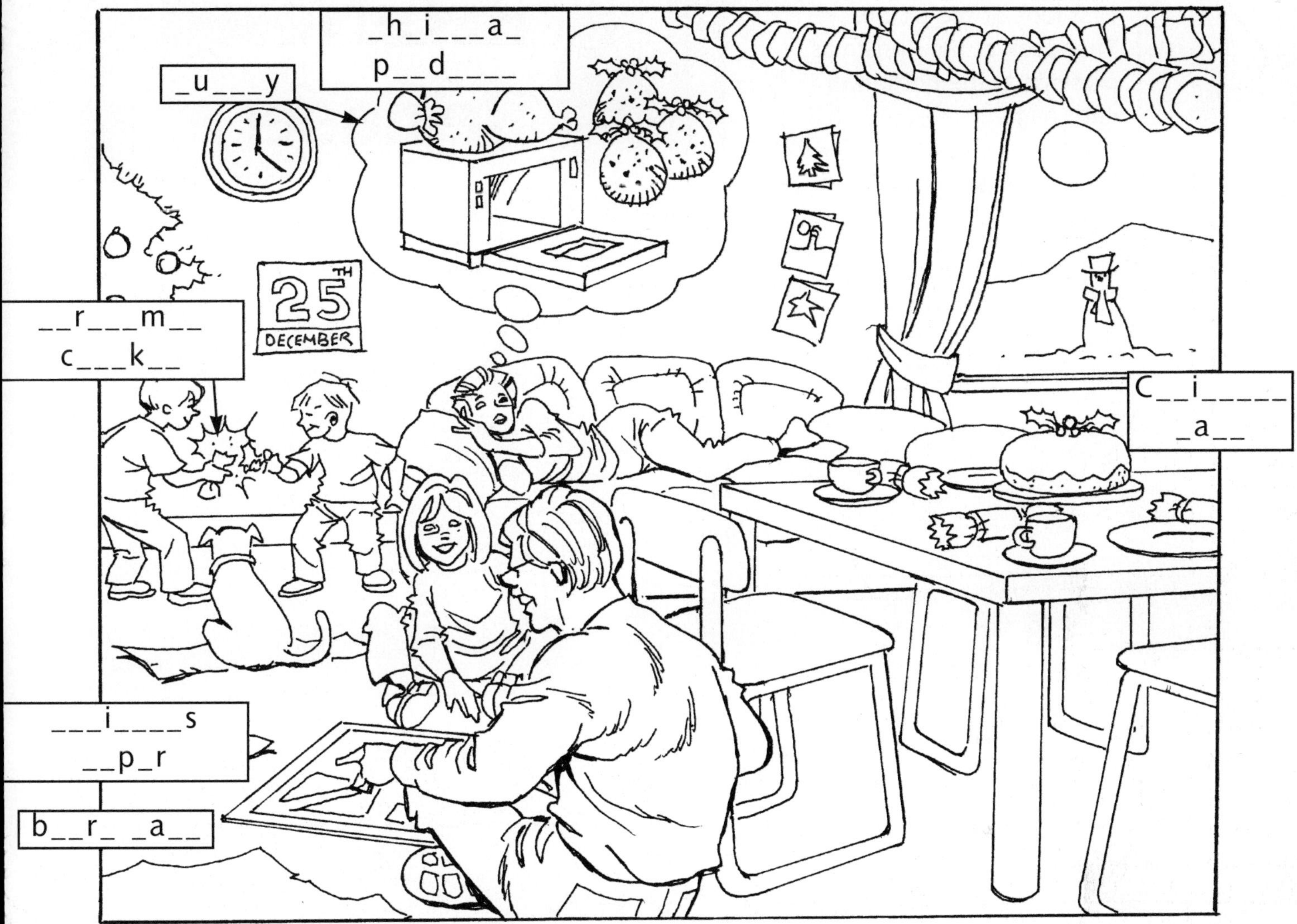

It's Christmas Day!
Everyone is in the living-room. There is Christmas paper everywhere!
Sally and Dad are playing a new board game. Sally is winning!

Mum is sleeping on the sofa. She is dreaming about the Christmas dinner.... She is in the kitchen.... The turkey is too big for the oven and there are lots of Christmas puddings!!!

Ben and Mark have got a Christmas cracker. They are pulling it. Be careful! BANG! Now Mum isn't sleeping.

Now it's time for some Christmas cake, a cup of tea and some more Christmas crackers.

Rudolph the Red-Nosed Reindeer

First look at the pictures.
Then look at the Christmas presents at the bottom of each page.
Now write the story of Rudolph the Red-Nosed Reindeer under the pictures.

1.

2.

3.

4.

But one little reindeer is hiding in a big toy box. His name is Rudolph.

It's Christmas Eve at the North Pole. Father Christmas and his helpers are in the toy factory.

Father Christmas must find eight strong reindeer to pull his sleigh. All the reindeer want to help him.

They are packing Christmas presents for all the boys and girls.

My red nose is terrible! I don't like it.

Dasher and Dancer, Prancer and Vixen, Comet and Cupid, Donder and Blitzen! That's eight reindeer.

5.

6.

HAPPY CHRISTMAS
FROM
FATHER CHRISTMAS

7.

8.

The helpers are putting the presents onto the sleigh.
He is very unhappy because he has got a bright red nose.
Father Christmas is writing names on the presents.

But it's getting dark and they can't see!

Father Christmas has a good idea. Rudolph can help to pull the sleigh.

Now Father Christmas and his reindeer are up in the sky. They are taking Christmas presents to all the boys and girls.

Suddenly there is a bright red light. It's Rudolph's shiny red nose.

Winter fun

Q: Where do snowmen dance?
A: At the snowball.

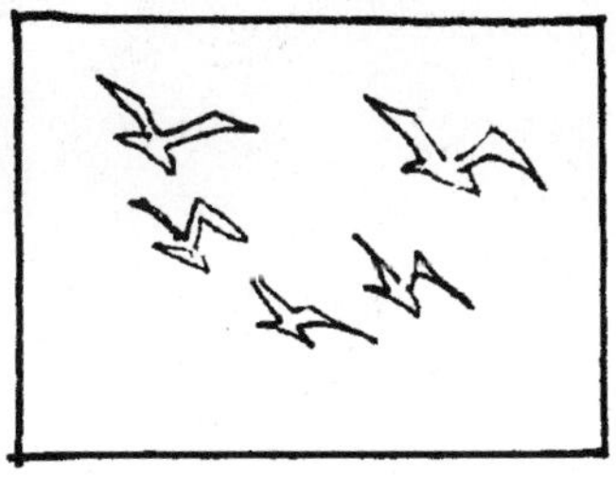

Q: Why do birds fly south in winter?
A: Because it's too far to walk.

Q: Why does a mother kangaroo hate winter?
A: Because her children must play inside.

Q: Why does Father Christmas wear red trousers?
A: Because his black trousers are at the cleaners.

I don't care who you are! Get those reindeer off my roof!

Teacher: Tell me an animal that lives in Lapland.
Pupil: A reindeer.
Teacher: Good! Now tell me one more.
Pupil: Er......, another reindeer!

Teacher: How do you spell 'CHRISTMAS'?
Pupil: K-R-I-S-S-M-A-S-S.
Teacher: The dictionary spells it 'C-H-R-I-S-T-M-A-S'.
Pupil: You didn't ask me how the dictionary spells it

Joey's Christmas Poem

Sing Christmas **C**arols!

Say 'Merry C**H**ristmas' to your Mum and Dad!

Look at your Christmas ca**R**ds!

Eat a big Christmas d**I**nner!

Open your Chri**S**tmas presents!

Make a **T**urkey sandwich! (And eat it!)

Play a Christmas ga**M**e with your Mum and Dad!

Pull a Christmas cr**A**cker with your brother!

Eat Chri**S**tmas cake for tea!

by Joey

Please read my Christmas poem on page 22 again.
Now write a poem on this page.
You can decorate the poem with little pictures, too. Don't forget your name!

My poem about Christmas

_______________ C _______________

_______________ H _______________

_______________ R _______________

_______________ I _______________

_______________ S _______________

_______________ T _______________

_______________ M _______________

_______________ A _______________

_______________ S _______________

Pancake Day - Shrove Tuesday

It's Shrove Tuesday.
Sally, Ben and Mark are making pancakes for the pancake race.
Read the recipe and then find and colour all the things they need in the kitchen.

PANCAKES

1. Sieve 125g of flour into a big bowl.
2. Add one egg and a pinch of salt. Mix together.
3. Add 250ml of milk and whisk together for about 5 minutes.
4. Slowly melt one teaspoon of butter in a non-stick frying-pan.
5. Pour 2 to 3 tablespoons of the pancake mixture into the frying-pan.
6. Cook the pancake on one side for about 3 minutes.
7. Now, if you can, toss the pancake up in the air and catch it in the pan and cook the other side. Good luck!
8. Put the cooked pancake on a warm plate.
9. You can eat the pancakes with lemon juice and sugar or with jam.

tea
flour
biscuits
1000
500
strawberry jam
salt
cocoa
ice box
margarine
butter
salami
cheese
honey

Don't forget Tim. You must toss the pancake 3 times.
Come on Danny!
Oh, bad luck Sally!
And the winner is Mrs Williams!
FINISH
Well done!
Hooray!

Springtime

Mrs Smith is Sally's English teacher. Today Mrs Smith is writing poems about springtime with Sally's class.

Read what Mrs Smith is saying and look at the four pictures and the words in the pictures. Now you can try to write a nice poem about springtime, too! Draw some nice pictures round your poem.

First write your words in three columns - like this. The three words must belong together, of course. For example: grey rabbits hopping, fluffy chicks hiding ...

Please find about eight more examples like these and write them down. Read your poem to your friend and draw some nice pictures to go with it.

It's Springtime

There are

grey rabbits hopping,
fluffy chicks hiding,

- It's springtime.

The Easter egg hunt

Here is a picture of the garden. Do you know where Dad's Easter eggs are? Look again at what Sally says and then draw and colour the eggs in the garden.

You can hide the five orange eggs for Dad.

Now write down where the eggs are.

There is one orange egg...

There are two orange eggs...

Another egg is...

____

____

____

____

____

____

The Easter bunny game

You can make and play this exciting board game.

But first you must make: a white Easter bunny,
a grey Easter bunny,
and six game strips.

Let's make the two Easter bunnies first!

1. Cut two paper strips (1.5cm by 7cm). Colour one strip grey - for the grey Easter bunny.

2. Bend the paper so that the ends meet and glue the ends together.

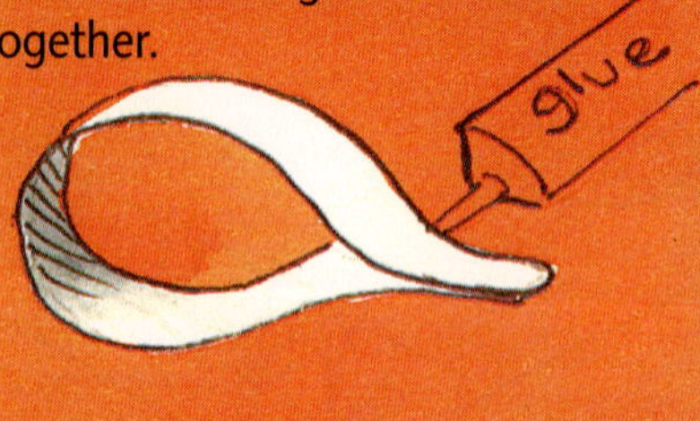

3. Cut off the corners to make the Easter bunny's head.

4. Draw two eyes, a nose, a mouth and whiskers with a black felt-tip pen.

5. Glue two pink ears and a little bobtail onto your bunnies.

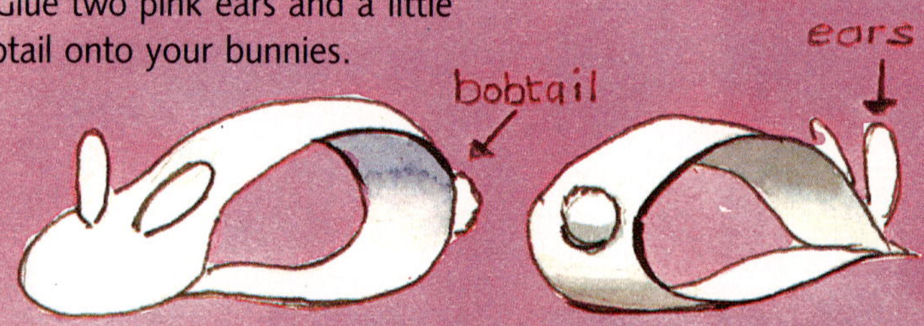

6. Now they are ready for the game.

Mother: Doctor, doctor, my little boy thinks he's a chicken!
Doctor: That's terrible! Why didn't you come to me earlier?
Mother: We needed the eggs!

The game strips

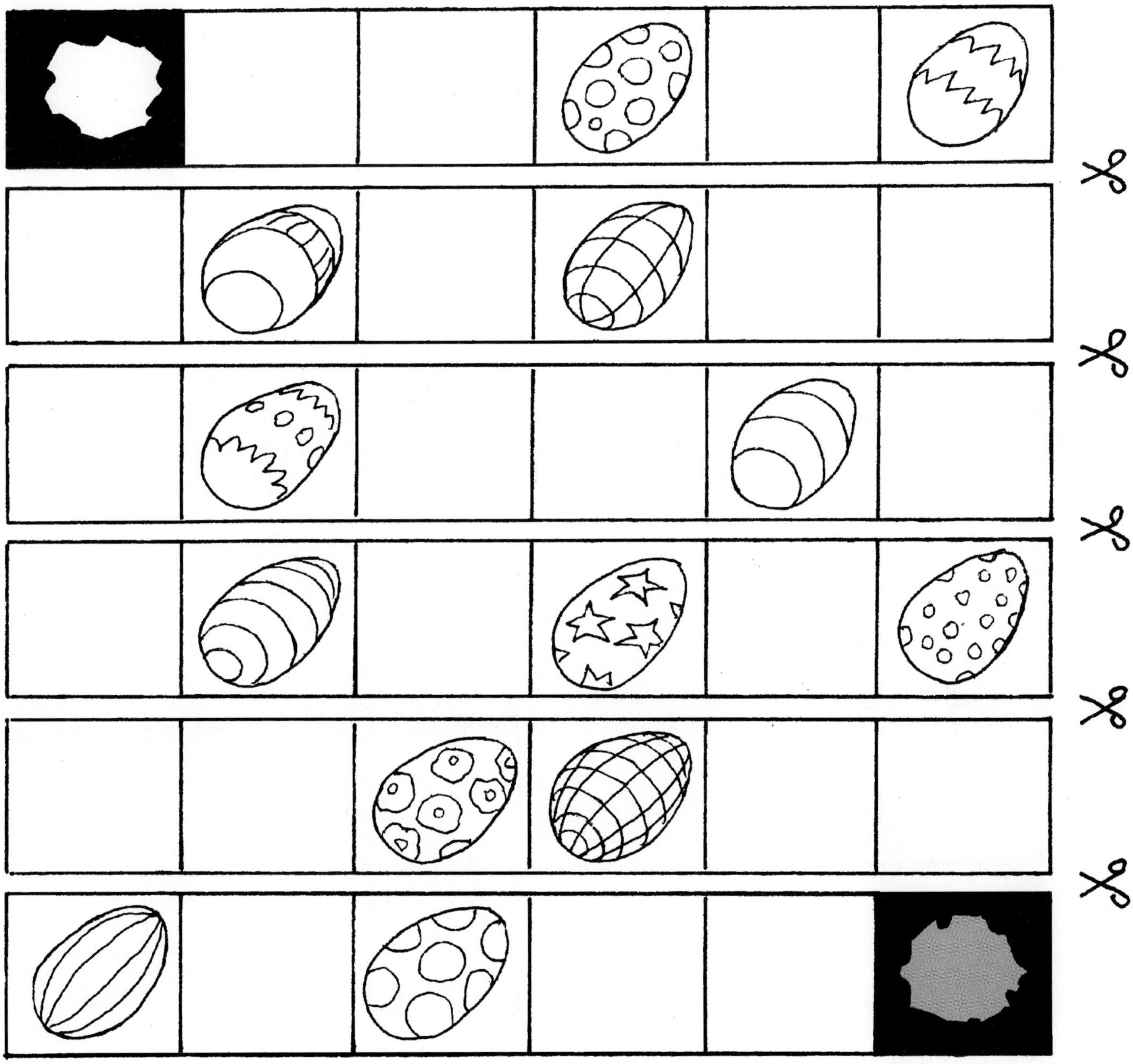

Is it true that carrots are good for your eyes?
Well, you never see rabbits with glasses.

1. Mix up the strips and make a field. The two rabbit holes must be at the corners.

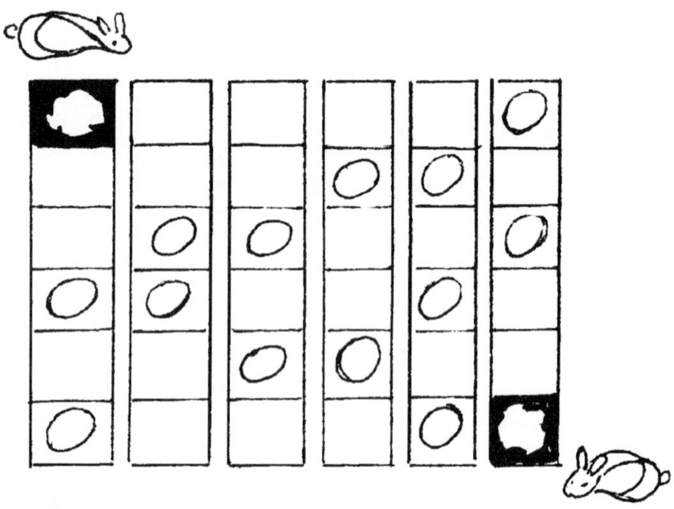

2. Put the grey Easter bunny on the grey rabbit hole and the white Easter bunny on the white rabbit hole.

3. Now the game can begin! Your bunny must hop from his rabbit hole to the other rabbit hole.

4. Now you can choose how to move your Easter bunny.

a) You can move one game strip up or down <u>one square</u> to make an 'Easter egg path'.

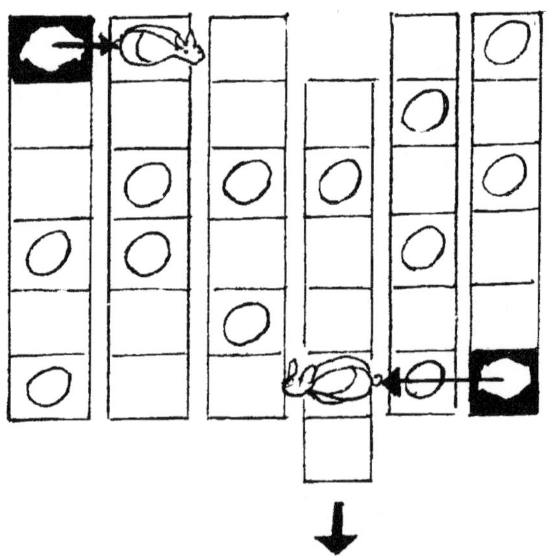

b) If you can't make an 'Easter egg path', you can only move your Easter bunny onto the next square.

IMPORTANT!

Your partner can't move the same game strip after you.

The rabbit can move up or down the field but not diagonally.

5. **The first rabbit on the other hole square is the winner!**

Summer holidays rap

Here's a summer holiday rap for you to learn with your class. Half the class can say the rap. The rest of the class can give the rap rhythm. You don't need any musical instruments - just your hands and feet!

Summer is here
and the sky is blue.
Holiday time
for me and for you.
No more school!

Meet your friends
at the swimming pool.
Dive in the water -
it's nice and cool.
Summertime!

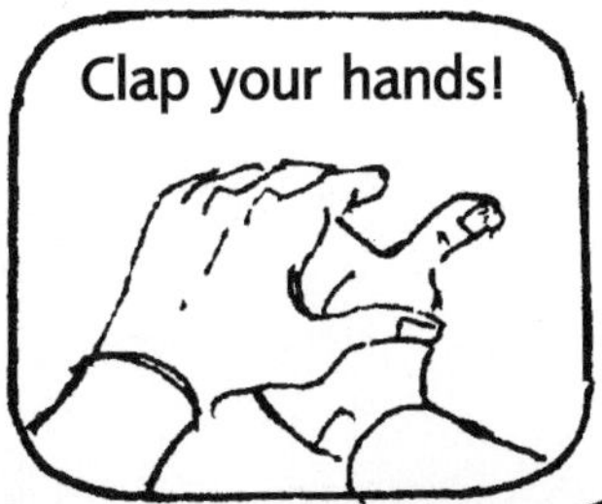

Inline skating
in the park.
Play till eight,
it isn't dark.
Long warm days.

It's time for a picnic
down by the lake.
Sandwiches, apples,
and chocolate cake.
Here come the wasps!

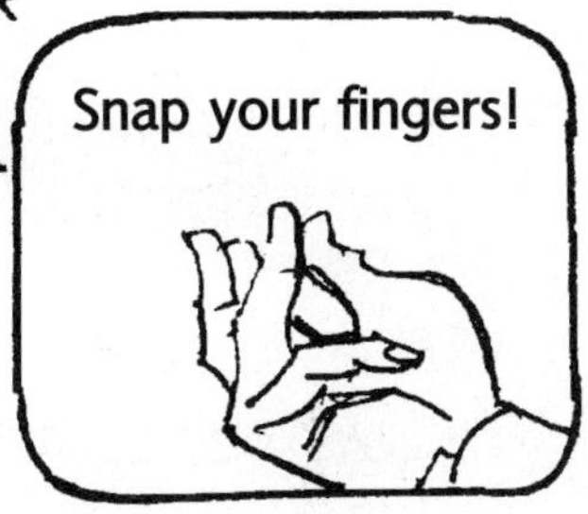

Visit the animals
at the zoo.
Tigers, elephants,
a kangaroo.
Oh, what fun!

Pack your bags.
Get in the car.
Off to the seaside.
It isn't far.
Holidays!

Go to the beach
and watch the ships.
Drink lemonade
and eat fish and chips
in the sun.

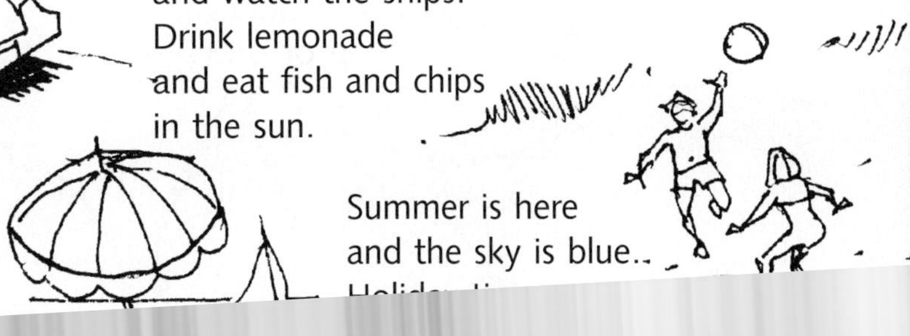

Summer is here
and the sky is blue..

At the

It's a lovely sunny day. There are lots of people having fun at the seaside.
What are they saying?
Look under the picture and find the right sentences. Then fill in the speech bubbles.

seaside

CARAVAN SITE
FUNFAIR
You can't play
Can I have an
Oooh! The
is cold!
caravan
Yuck! There's sand in my sandwich!

A Holiday Adventure

First look at these pictures. Then read the story on page 37.

What do you think the people are saying? Fill in the speech bubbles!

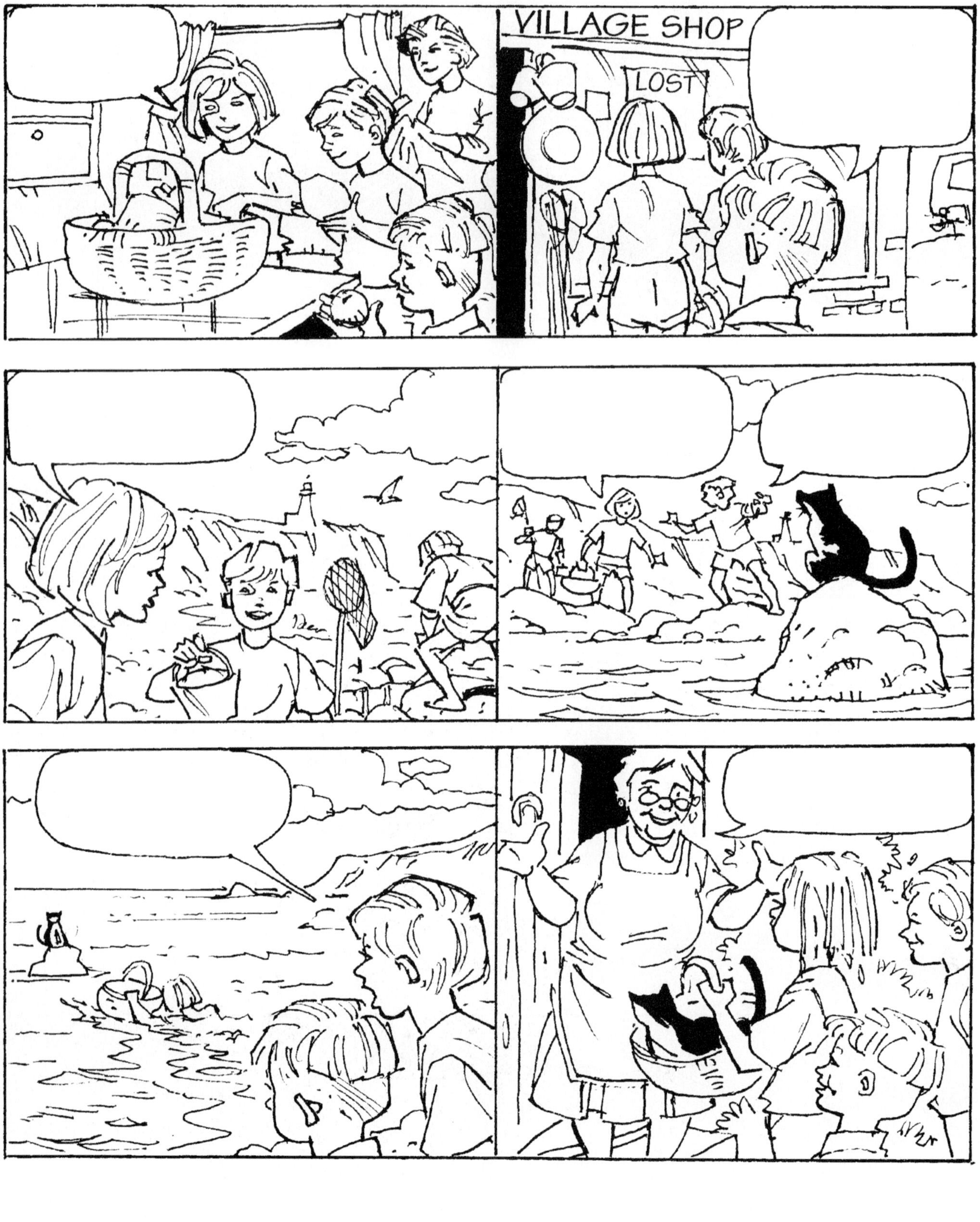

A Holiday Adventure

Sally's family has got a caravan. Every summer they take their caravan to a caravan site near the sea. This summer they are staying at a caravan site in Sandy Bay.

It's Sunday morning. Sally, Ben and Mark get up early. They put on their swimming things, pack a picnic in a big basket and get their fishing things. Then they say goodbye to Mum, Dad and Spot the dog.

On the way to the beach, they walk past the village shop. They stop and look in the window. There's a big poster. It says:

> LOST
>
> A black and white cat
>
> Mrs Davids, Rose Cottage
>
> Sandy Bay

Soon they are on the beach. They walk over the sand till they come to some rocks. They climb over the rocks and find a good place to stop. They get out their fishing nets and begin to fish. Sally and Ben are unlucky. Mark catches one little fish, but he throws it back into the sea. At 12 o'clock everyone is hungry, so they unpack the picnic basket and eat all their food. It's delicious!

After lunch they climb over the rocks and look for interesting shells and stones. Suddenly they hear a funny sound not far away. They climb towards the sound. What can it be? The sound gets louder and louder. It comes from a big rock in the sea. Then suddenly Ben sees something move on the rock. It's black and white. It's a cat. It must be the lost cat! It's stranded on the rock and it can't get back.

Sally quickly empties the picnic basket and jumps into the sea. She wants to rescue the cat. The water is very deep and she has to swim. She holds the basket over the water with one hand and swims with the other. It's hard work. Soon she arrives at the rock and climbs up to the cat. She puts it into the basket and climbs back down again. She swims with the cat in the basket back to Mark and Ben.

Half an hour later they are at Rose Cottage. They ring the doorbell and Mrs Davids opens the door. She's very happy when she sees her cat. She thanks the children. Then she gives the cat something to eat and makes a delicious 'thank-you-tea' for the children.

Who is who at the swimming pool?

Betty is sitting between Janet and Mandy.
Cathy, Mandy and Betty have got sunglasses.
Tammy, Betty and Janet are wearing sun hats.
Mandy, Becky and Betty are reading.
Mandy and Cathy aren't drinking lemonade.
Cathy,Tammy and Janet are eating ice-creams.

Girl number 1 is ______________________________.

Girl number 2 is ______________________________.

Girl number 3 is ______________________________.

Girl number 4 is ______________________________.

Girl number 5 is ______________________________.

Girl number 6 is ______________________________.

Answer on page 40.

Arbeitsaufträge

Can you complete the sentences?	Kannst du die Sätze zu Ende schreiben?
Colour the picture.	Male das Bild aus.
Complete the words.	Vervollständige die Wörter.
Decorate the ...	Schmücke den/die/das ...
Draw some pictures.	Male einige Bilder.
Fill in the speech bubbles.	Schreibe die Texte in die Sprechblasen.
Find about eight more examples.	Finde etwa acht weitere Beispiele
Find the right sentence.	Finde den richtigen Satz.
Finish the picture.	Male das Bild zu Ende.
Look at the pictures.	Sieh dir die Bilder an.
Match the verses to the pictures.	Ordne die Strophen den Bildern zu.
Now play the game with your classmates.	Spiele jetzt das Spiel mit deinen KlassenkameradInnen.
Read the notes on the pinboard.	Lies die Notizen auf der Pinwand.
Read the poem.	Lies das Gedicht.
The words are underlined in the text.	Die Wörter sind im Text unterstrichen.
The words must belong to each other.	Die Wörter müssen zusammen passen.
Try to write ...	Versuche ... zu schreiben
Write the story.	Schreibe die Geschichte.
Write the story under the picture.	Schreibe die Geschichte unter die Bilder.
Write your words in three columns.	Schreibe deine Wörter in drei Spalten.

Birthdays

balloons	Luftballons
blindfold	Augenbinde
cake	Kuchen
candles	Kerzen
drawing-pin	Reißbrettstift
Happy birthday to you!	Herzlichen Glückwunsch zum Geburtstag!
head	Kopf
How old are you today?	Wie alt wirst du heute?
It's my birthday today.	Heute ist mein Geburtstag.
It's your turn.	Du bist dran.
jelly	Wackelpudding
Let's play ...	Lasst uns ... spielen.
Let's sing ...	Lasst uns ... singen.
party game	Partyspiel
plate	Teller
presents	Geschenke
Turn Sally!	Drehe/Dreht Sally im Kreis herum!

Halloween

bat	Fledermaus
to be frightened	ängstlich sein
to bend	biegen
broomstick	Besenstiel
cape	Umhang
corner	Ecke
crown	Krone
to cut	schneiden
dark	dunkel
dress	Kleid
ears	Ohren
eyes	Augen
face	Gesicht
to fold	falten
frightened	ängstlich
ghost	Gespenst
glue	Klebstoff
golden	golden
hair	Haare
to hide behind a bush	sich hinter einem Busch verstecken
hole	Loch
knitting needle	Stricknadel
Knock on the door.	Klopfe/Klopft an die Tür.
to laugh	lachen
material	Stoff, Material
mouth	Mund
nose	Nase
pumpkin	Kürbis
to push through	durchstechen
scissors	Schere
sharp knitting needle	spitze Stricknadel
sheet	Bettlaken
Shout 'Trick or treat!'	Rufe/Ruft 'Streiche oder Süßigkeiten'.
soft material	weicher Stoff
spooky	unheimlich
sweets	Süßigkeiten
tail	Schwanz
teeth	Zähne
to tie	zusammenbinden
thread	Nähgarn
tonight	heute Abend
Trick or treat	Streiche oder Süßigkeiten
trousers	Hose
to wear	tragen (Kleidung)
wings	Flügel
wire clothes hanger	Kleiderbügel aus Draht
witch	Hexe

Christmas

another	noch ein/e/er
at the cleaners	in der Reinigung
to bark	bellen
bird	Vogel
board game	Brettspiel
bright red light	helles, rotes Licht
ceiling	Decke
chimney	Schornstein
Christmas carols	Weihnachtslieder
Christmas cracker	Knallbonbon
Christmas Day	1. Weihnachtstag
Christmas dinner	Weihnachtsessen
Christmas Eve	Heiligabend
Christmas pudding	kuchenartige, süße Nachspeise
Christmas stocking	Weihnachtsstrumpf
Christmas tree	Christbaum
coloured fairy lights	bunte Lichterkette
cup of tea	Tasse Tee
to dance	tanzen
dictionary	Wörterbuch
downstairs	im Erdgeschoss
to dream	träumen
everyone	alle
everywhere	überall
Father Christmas	Weihnachtsmann
to fly	fliegen
He got stuck.	Er ist steckengeblieben.

to hide	sich verstecken
kitchen	Küche
light	Licht
living-room	Wohnzimmer
paper-chains	Papiergirlanden
to play inside	drinnen spielen
pretty	hübsch
to pull	ziehen
reindeer	Rentier/e
sky	Himmel
sleigh	Schlitten
to spell	buchstabieren
strong	stark
tea	Tee
too far	zu weit
toy factory	Spielzeugfabrik
turkey	Truthahn
unhappy	unglücklich
upstairs	im ersten Stock
wall	Wand
What bad luck!	Was für ein Pech!
to win	gewinnen
You didn't ask me … .	Sie haben mich nicht gefragt …

Pancake Day

to add	hinzufügen
a pinch of salt	eine Prise Salz
bowl	Schüssel
to catch	auffangen
to cook a pancake	einen Pfannkuchen backen
egg	Ei
finish	Ziel(linie)
flour	Mehl
jam	Marmelade
kitchen	Küche
lemon juice	Zitronensaft
to melt slowly	langsam schmelzen lassen
milk	Milch
to need	brauchen
non-stick frying pan	kunststoffbeschichtete Bratpfanne
pancake mixture	Pfannkuchenteig
pancakes	Pfannkuchen
to pour	gießen
race	Wettrennen
recipe	Kochrezept
Shrove Tuesday	Fastnachtsdienstag
to sieve	(durch)sieben
start	Start(linie)
tablespoon	Eßlöffel
teaspoon	Teelöffel
to toss the pancake in the air	den Pfannkuchen hochwerfen und wenden
to whisk together	Zutaten zusammen rühren

Springtime

beautiful	(wunder)schön
bees	Bienen
birds	Vögel
buds	Knospen
to buzz	summen
chicks	Küken
Close your eyes!	Schließe deine/ Schließt eure Augen!
clouds	Wolken
flowers	Blumen
fluffy	flauschig
lambs	Lämmer
of course	natürlich, sicher
rabbits	Kaninchen
springtime	Frühlingszeit
tulips	Tulpen

Easter

basket	Korb
bobtail	Häschenschwanz
bunny	Häschen
to come back again	wieder zurückkommen
to copy	kopieren
Easter egg hunt	Ostereiersuche
garden shed	Gartenhäuschen
hiding place	Versteck
important	wichtig
to look out the window	aus dem Fenster schauen
to mix up	mischen
to move diagonally	diagonal ziehen
on the left/right	links/rechts
paper strips	Papierstreifen
pond	Gartenteich
rabbit hole	Kaninchenbau
rabbit hutch	Kaninchenstall
sandpit	Sandkasten
square	Kästchen
thick card	stabiler Karton
to turn left/right	links/rechts abbiegen
to walk down the garden path	den Gartenweg hinuntergehen
whiskers	Schnurrhaare
You can choose how to move … .	Du kannst dir aussuchen, wie du … bewegen willst.

Summer

adventure	Abenteuer
at the seaside	am Meer
beach	Strand
caravan site	Campingplatz
to climb	klettern
deep	tief
delicious	lecker
to dive	tauchen
to empty	ausleeren
fish and chips	Backfisch mit Pommes
funfair	Vergnügungspark
funny sound	seltsames Geräusch
inline skating	Inlineskaten
It is hard work.	Es ist anstrengend (harte Arbeit).
lake	See
lost	verloren
to move	sich bewegen
pier	Pier
to rescue	retten
to ring the doorbell	an der Tür klingeln
rock	Felsen
sea	Meer
shells	Muscheln
sound	Geräusch, Ton
stranded	gestrandet
swimming things	Schwimmsachen
to throw back	wieder hineinwerfen
to walk past	vorbeigehen
wasps	Wespen

Answers for page 38.
1. Janet 2. Betty 3. Mandy 4. Becky 5. Tammy 6. Cathy